Bearded Dragon Facts for Kids

Explore the Fascinating World of Pogonas and Learn Everything You Need to Know About Them

© **Copyright 2024 - All rights reserved.**

The content contained within this book may not be reproduced, duplicated, or transmitted without direct written permission from the author or the publisher.

Under no circumstances will any blame or legal responsibility be held against the publisher or author for any damages, reparation, or monetary loss due to the information contained within this book, either directly or indirectly.

Legal Notice:

This book is copyright-protected. It is only for personal use. You cannot amend, distribute, sell, use, quote, or paraphrase any part of the content within this book without the consent of the author or publisher.

Disclaimer Notice:

Please note the information contained within this document is for educational and entertainment purposes only. All effort has been executed to present accurate, up-to-date, reliable, and complete information. No warranties of any kind are declared or implied. Readers acknowledge that the author is not engaging in the rendering of legal, financial, medical, or professional advice. The content within this book has been derived from various sources. Please consult a licensed professional before attempting any techniques outlined in this book.

By reading this document, the reader agrees that under no circumstances is the author responsible for any losses, direct or indirect, that are incurred as a result of the use of the information contained within this document, including, but not limited to, errors, omissions, or inaccuracies.

Table of Contents

Introduction 1

Chapter 1: Introduction 3

Chapter 2: Meet the Bearded Dragon 13

**Chapter 3: Setting Up the Perfect
Bearded Dragon Home** 22

Chapter 4: Feeding and Nutrition 29

Chapter 5: Health and Wellness 37

Chapter 6: Fun Facts and Quirky Behavior 45

Chapter 7: Engaging Activities for Kids 52

Chapter 8: Frequently Asked Questions 62

Conclusion 69

References 71

Introduction

The name "bearded dragon" will make anyone think twice. Is it a real thing? Do they exist? You may even start racking your brains to remember which folk tale they are from. You may not find them in fiction books, but they can indeed be found in nonfiction books on the animal kingdom. Yes, bearded dragons are as real as dogs or cats.

But what are these bearded dragons? Are they really dragons? How big are they? If they are like dogs or cats, can they be taken in as pets? Are they friendly or violent by nature? This book will answer all these questions and more. You will find everything there is to know about the fascinating world of bearded dragons here.

Do they breathe fire? Are they as frighteningly magnificent as the fairy tales say they are? Do they really have a beard? Everything from their eating habits to their living conditions will be explained in vivid detail. This book isn't like the other books where you need to refer to the dictionary in each sentence. It is written in simple language since it focuses on understanding bearded dragons.

Even if you are new to the world of animals and pets (bearded dragons may sound like highly advanced, mythic creatures), you will be able to understand and follow everything in the book, from recreating the dragon's environment at home to caring for it. It also includes a number of fun facts and activities near the end.

Chapter 1: Introduction

Bearded dragons are called not because they are actually dragons. They don't walk or talk like those mythical creatures. They don't sprout wings or breathe fire, either. Dragons are a part of human imagination, but in the fictional universe, they are a part of the "lizard" family tree. Which is what bearded dragons are - lizards. But they aren't just any lizard. They are huge creatures with hefty bodies and long tails. Their most interesting characteristic is that they sport beards. More importantly, they aren't harmful like most other lizards but friendly and playful, making them perfect pets for children.

1. *Bearded dragon side profile. Source: Jpkaiser2, CC BY-SA 4.0 <https://creativecommons.org/licenses/by-sa/4.0>, via Wikimedia Commons. https://commons.wikimedia.org/wiki/File:2_bearded_dragons_sitting_together.jpg*

Brief Overview of Bearded Dragons

"Bearded dragon" isn't the official name of these reptiles. It's a nickname. Scientists call them pogonas, which is a family (genus) of eight lizard species. Looking at a pogona from afar, you would think it has a thick, long beard on its chin. That is how it got the nickname "bearded dragon." However, the beard-like growth isn't full of hair. It is a crop of spikes and scales, which you see once you touch the underside of its throat.

What is even stranger is they can change the color of their beard or make it grow at a moment's notice. It's their communication method or a response to certain situations. When their beard turns black, it probably means they feel threatened or stressed. In these cases, they may also puff up their throat, giving the impression of growing their beard. If there is a female dragon in the vicinity, the chances are your male dragon is trying to attract her attention by showing off his magnificent beard.

Bearded dragons come in almost every color imaginable, from dark black to bright white. Red, orange, yellow, and many other colored species are also found. Their length differentiates them from other lizards since they may often grow up to a whopping 24 inches. They usually feed on small insects and certain veggies.

Pogonas are originally from Australia, so they prefer a dry, arid climate. They bask in the sun during the day, generally perched atop a rock or an elevated surface, and sleep soundly in a burrowed hole in the ground at night. However, they cannot survive in extreme temperatures. They will flourish in temperatures between 60°F and 80°F. Their lifespan is usually around 10 years, but they may even live to 15-17 years with proper care.

Why Bearded Dragons Make Great Pets for Kids

2. Bearded dragons are known for their calm and gentle demeanor. Source: LBJ Library from Austin, Public domain, via Wikimedia Commons. https://commons.wikimedia.org/wiki/File:LBJ_Foundation_DIG1 4061-90_(33927841121).jpg

Did you know that bearded dragons were first introduced to the United States in the 1990s? They became an instant success with kids and adults, and since then, their demand has risen. They were, and still are, seen as exotic pets. So, if you own a bearded dragon, you might just be crowned the leader of your pet group. If you are apprehensive about owning one as a kid, here are a few good facts to help you change your mind.

- **Docile Nature:**

    Bearded dragons are known for their calm and gentle demeanor. They are generally more tolerant of handling than other reptiles. Their laid-back nature makes them suitable for children who want a pet they can interact with.

- **Manageable Size:**

    Bearded dragons are medium-sized reptiles (around 20 inches long), making them more manageable for kids than larger species. Their size allows for easier handling and care, and they don't require as much space as some reptiles.

- **Low Maintenance:**

    While proper care is crucial, bearded dragons are considered relatively low-maintenance pets. They don't have complex diets, and their habitat setup is more straightforward than that of other reptiles. This can be appealing if you own a pet for the first time.

- **Educational Opportunities:**

    Keeping a bearded dragon can be a valuable educational experience. Caring for a living creature teaches responsibility, time management, and the importance of meeting another living being's needs. It also teaches about biology, ecology, and the natural behaviors of lizards.

- **Social Interaction:**

    Bearded dragons can form bonds with their owners and often enjoy human interaction. They may tolerate gentle handling and can be responsive to their owners. This social aspect can be rewarding for kids, fostering companionship and responsibility.

- **Fascinating Behavior:**

    Bearded dragons exhibit interesting behaviors, like head bobbing, arm waving, and puffing up their beard during displays. Observing these behaviors can entertain and educate children, sparking curiosity about the natural world.

- **Long Lifespan:**

    When cared for properly, bearded dragons can live for many years (10-15 years). Your bearded dragon can be a long-term companion for most of your childhood.

- **Therapeutic Benefits:**

    Interacting with pets, including bearded dragons, can be therapeutic. Caring for and spending time with a pet can reduce stress, provide comfort, and improve your well-being.

- **Less Allergic:**

    Humans are sometimes allergic to animal fur or hair. These allergies are often found in children. Cats and dogs don't really make ideal pets in that regard due to their abundant hair. Although bearded dragons are named so, they do not have a beard, hair, or fur. Therefore, there is a low possibility of you being allergic to them.

Owning a bearded dragon as a pet has many advantages, but there is also one possible con. Like other reptiles, pogonas also carry the salmonella bacteria in their feces (poop). It can be harmful if you come in contact with this bacteria. You may have a fever, stomach cramps, or diarrhea for several days, but it will eventually go away.

Another point to note is its bite. When bearded dragons feel threatened, they not only puff up and change their beard color, but they may also bite you. Though their bite is poisonous, you don't have to worry. It is a mild poison that won't affect you in any way. At most, their bite may cause a tiny puncture wound on your skin, like from a needle. Simply clean the wound and wash your hands to prevent bacteria buildup.

Importance of Understanding and Caring for Bearded Dragons

Bearded dragons are solitary creatures (they like being on their own). Unlike other pets, they don't demand constant attention and handling. Nonetheless, they can be very social and playful sometimes, making them ideal pets for first-timers. However, you must understand their behavior and care for them to help them live a long and happy life.

3. *A bearded dragon that's happy to see you! Source: Obolton (talk) (Uploads), Public domain, via Wikimedia Commons.*

https://commons.wikimedia.org/wiki/File:Bearded_Dragon_showing_beard.jpg

- **Animal Welfare:**

    Responsible pet ownership means meeting the needs of the animals you care for. Understanding bearded dragons' natural behaviors, diet, and environmental needs is essential for a suitable and enriching life.

- **Health Maintenance:**

    Proper care helps prevent health issues in bearded dragons, such as metabolic bone disease, respiratory infections, and parasites. Regular vet check-ups, a balanced diet, and proper temperatures and lighting conditions improve their health and longevity.

- **Educational Value:**

    Keeping bearded dragons is an educational opportunity for you. Learning about the biology, behavior, and habitat of these reptiles can create a deeper appreciation for the natural world and your understanding of ecosystems and life sciences.

- **Promoting Responsible Pet Ownership:**

    Understanding the commitment to caring for bearded dragons promotes responsible pet ownership. It encourages you to make the right decisions, invest time and proper care, and consider the long-term commitment to your pet's well-being.

- **Positive Interaction:**

    Bearded dragons can form lasting bonds. Understanding their behaviors and preferences allows positive interaction, strengthening the owner-pet relationship. This interaction can be emotionally fulfilling for you and your pet.

- **Behavioral Observation:**

    Bearded dragons have amazingly cute behavior. Beard puffing aside, they also bob their head or wave their hands. Understanding these behaviors helps you interpret their mood, health, and communication signals so you have a healthier and more interactive relationship.

- **Environmental Enrichment:**

    An enriched environment for the mental and physical health of bearded dragons is essential. It includes creating a habitat with hiding spots, climbing opportunities, and objects for exploration. Enrichment activities stimulate their brain, like rearranging the habitat or introducing novel items.

- **Species Conservation:**

    Learning about bearded dragons' natural habitat and conservation raises awareness about the importance of preserving their ecosystems. Since the Australian government has banned the export of pogonas, the species you receive will have been bred in the US, so you won't need special conditions for its conservation. Nevertheless, supporting responsible breeding practices and avoiding the illegal trade of wild-caught specimens helps preserve these reptiles.

- **Community Engagement:**

    Knowing about bearded dragons lets you share information with others in the pet community. Sharing helps promote the best practices for these creatures, so this useful knowledge exchange will help you take better care of your pet. This useful exchange of knowledge will also help you take better care of your pet.

Chapter 2: Meet the Bearded Dragon

Now that you have a general idea about a bearded dragon and why it is the right pet for you, it's time to dive into this fascinating creature's character. When you say "bearded dragon" or its biological name, "pogona," you are referring to its genus (a biological classification) rather than the animal.

4. *A bearded dragon is a unique type of lizard. Source: Cliomd1, CC BY-SA 4.0 <https://creativecommons.org/licenses/by-sa/4.0>, via Wikimedia Commons. https://commons.wikimedia.org/wiki/File:Juvenile_bearded_dragon.jpg*

What makes this genus of lizards different from others of its kind? What are the unique traits that make it stand apart in the animal kingdom? In which climatic conditions does it thrive? What makes them ideal pets? This chapter covers these questions and more as you meet and get to know your bearded dragon for the first time.

Physical Characteristics

When you see a bearded dragon, you can easily see it is a lizard. It has various characteristics that define a lizard: a long tail, four V-shaped limbs, a thick cylindrical body, and a pointed head. However, pogonas are much longer in size than regular house lizards and reptiles. They usually grow up to 18 to 24 inches.

Bearded dragons have a stout, flattened body covered in tough, spiny scales. These scales are often in rows along their sides and back. They have triangular-shaped heads with a distinctive row of spiked scales along their throat and chin. Their four short limbs with five clawed toes on each foot are well-adapted for climbing and digging. Their long, muscular tail makes up most of their overall length.

Bearded dragons come in various colors, including shades of brown, tan, yellow, orange, and sometimes red or even black. Some may have patterns or markings, like stripes or spots. Their eyes are large and round with vertically slit pupils. Apart from these, they have a few unique characteristics that make bearded dragons unique.

Unique Features
- Beard Puffing: One of the most distinctive features of bearded dragons is how they puff out their throat and

chin, creating a "beard" of spiky scales. They do this to appear larger and more intimidating when threatened or during territorial displays.

5. *Bearded dragon puffing its beard. Source: Trent Townsend, CC BY 3.0 <https://creativecommons.org/licenses/by/3.0>, via Wikimedia Commons.*
https://commons.wikimedia.org/wiki/File:Eastern_Bearded_Dra gon_defence.JPG

- **Third Eye:** Bearded dragons have a parietal eye, or a "third eye." This eye is located on the top of their head and is not used for seeing like their proper eyes. Instead, it's sensitive to changes in light and helps regulate their circadian rhythm (natural processes during 24 hours) and detect predators from above.

- **Tail Wagging:** While not unique to bearded dragons, they are known for their characteristic tail-wagging behavior. They may wag their tails as communication, signaling submission, curiosity, or even excitement.

- **Social Behavior:** They exhibit complex social behaviors, especially during the breeding season. Males may engage in head bobbing, arm waving, and "push-up" displays to establish dominance and attract females.

- **Regeneration:** Bearded dragons can regenerate lost or damaged tails, albeit not as perfectly as other reptiles. While the regenerated tail may not be identical to the original, it can still function normally.

- **Omni-Dentition:** Bearded dragons have a peculiar dental structure known as omni-dentition, meaning they have different types of teeth in their mouth. They have sharp teeth in the front for gripping and tearing prey and flatter teeth toward the back of their mouth for grinding plant matter.

6. *Bearded dragons' teeth. Source: Kitenutuk, CC BY-SA 3.0 <http://creativecommons.org/licenses/by-sa/3.0/>, via Wikimedia Commons.*
https://commons.wikimedia.org/wiki/File:Bearded_dragon_showing_his_teeth.jpg

- **Thermoregulation Behavior:** Bearded dragons exhibit interesting thermoregulation behavior. They bask in the sun or under heat lamps to raise their body temperature and then retreat to cooler areas to regulate it. They will change their body posture to expose more or less of their body surface to heat or shade.

Size and Lifespan

Not all bearded dragons grow up to 24 inches. Their size depends on their gender. Many males (not all) can reach 24 inches, but the females can grow no more than 20 inches. Baby dragons are around 3-4 inches long and can grow another four inches during the first few months. After that, their growth is steady as it may take years to reach their longest size.

Out in the wild, the lifespan of bearded dragons is much less. They usually die within 10 years because they are eaten by many animals, including birds, foxes, snakes, and other reptiles. The unavailability of enough food also adds to their early death. On the other hand, pet dragons can live up to 15 years (even longer) because they are better cared for in a home environment without any predators.

Habitat in the Wild

Because bearded dragons live longer as pets doesn't mean their wild habitat is too harsh. They hail from the arid (dry) regions of Australia but can be found in the southeastern areas of Asia, too. While they thrive in an arid climate, they don't mind semi-arid regions that don't receive much rainfall. They usually inhabit deserts, shrublands, woodlands, and dry forests.

- **Desert and Arid Regions:** These habitats typically have sparse vegetation, rocky outcrops, sandy soils, and limited water sources.
- **Shrublands and Grasslands:** Here, the vegetation may be more abundant than in deserts, but it is still sparse. These habitats provide some cover and foraging opportunities.
- **Rocky Outcrops and Crevices:** Bearded dragons are adept climbers and often seek shelter in rocky outcrops, crevices, and hollow logs. These are hiding places from predators and shelter from extreme temperatures.
- **Sun-Basking Sites:** You may know that humans generate heat internally to maintain body temperature. You are an endothermic being. Bearded dragons are ectothermic (cold-blooded) creatures, meaning they rely on external heat sources to regulate their body temperature (they cannot generate heat internally). They bask in the sun, typically from perches or rocks, to get the necessary heat.
- **Variety of Vegetation:** While bearded dragons inhabit arid environments, they are not only found in barren landscapes. They often live in areas with low-growing vegetation, like grasses, shrubs, and small trees for food and shelter.
- **Water Sources:** Although bearded dragons are adapted to arid conditions and get most of their water from their diet, they still need access to water sources. They can be found near water sources like creeks, waterholes, or areas with dew accumulation in the wild.

Common Varieties of Bearded Dragons

Eight species of bearded dragons are found. However, they are bred in captivity in the US. It's not as harsh as it sounds. Captive breeding is a scientific term for breeding various animals in controlled environments, so they grow up healthier and stronger than usual. Due to the captive breeding of bearded dragons, more than eight varieties are found today. The most common ones include:

- **Central Bearded Dragon (Pogona vitticeps):** This is the most common and widely recognized bearded dragon species in the pet trade. They are native to the central regions of Australia and typically tan to brown in color with patches of lighter or darker shades. Central bearded dragons are known for their friendly disposition and ease of care, explaining why they are so popular as pets.

7. *Central bearded dragon. Source: George Chernilevsky, Public domain, via Wikimedia Commons.*
https://commons.wikimedia.org/wiki/File:Pogona_vitticeps_close-up_2009_G2.jpg

- **Eastern Bearded Dragon (Pogona barbata):** Known as the familiar bearded dragon, the Eastern bearded dragon is found in the eastern regions of Australia. They are similar in appearance to central bearded dragons, but their head is narrower, and their scales are more pointed and spine-like. Eastern bearded dragons are known for their calm temperament.

8. *Eastern Bearded Dragon. Source: DiverDave, CC BY-SA 3.0 <https://creativecommons.org/licenses/by-sa/3.0>, via Wikimedia Commons. https://commons.wikimedia.org/wiki/File:Pogona_barbata-03.JPG*

- **Rankin's Dragon (Pogona henrylawsoni):** Rankin's dragons are smaller than central and eastern bearded dragons. They have a similar appearance to other bearded dragons but are usually more brightly colored with distinct banding patterns. Rankin's dragons are also known for their calm demeanor.

9. *Rankin's Dragon. Source: No machine-readable author provided. Magalhães assumed (based on copyright claims)., Public domain, via Wikimedia Commons.*
https://commons.wikimedia.org/wiki/File:Pogona_henrylawsoni.jpg

- **Dwarf Bearded Dragon (Pogona minor):** You may have already guessed that dwarf bearded dragons are the smallest. They are smaller versions of central and eastern bearded dragons with similar characteristics – probably why they are less common in the pet trade than other varieties.

10. *Dwarf Bearded Dragon. Source: Benny Trapp, CC BY-SA 4.0 <https://creativecommons.org/licenses/by-sa/4.0>, via Wikimedia Commons.*
https://commons.wikimedia.org/wiki/File:BennyTrapp_Pogona_minor.jpg

Chapter 3: Setting Up the Perfect Bearded Dragon Home

Anna loved to be at home. By the time the school bell rings, she is giddy and ready to go. She's always the first person outside the school, waiting for the school bus to take her home. The ride doesn't take up much space in her mind because she's already thinking of her room, bed, TV, her parents, and dinner. Whenever the bus stops at the front of her house, the sigh that leaves her lips is always deep and relieved.

Like with people, every animal has a home.

11. Bearded dragons in their home. Source: JefferyGoldman, CC BY-SA 4.0 <https://creativecommons.org/licenses/by-sa/4.0>, via Wikimedia Commons.
https://commons.wikimedia.org/wiki/File:Bearded_Dragons.jpg

Now, imagine for a moment that Anna no longer has a home to go to one day. How do you think she'll feel? Sad, right? So, it is too for animals. Like every other animal, your little friend, the bearded dragon, needs a home. A safe space where it can feel free and relieved from stress. These fascinating reptiles have a very unique appearance; they can't be seen just anywhere. Where's the class in that?

Putting together a home for your pet is one of the most exciting things about getting a bearded dragon. The task can be thrilling and overwhelming sometimes, so if you're ready to learn how to set up the perfect bearded dragon home, keep on reading. In this chapter, you'll be equipped with the tools and tips to ensure your pet has a home to call their own.

Creating the Ideal Terrarium

Don't let that big fancy word 'Terrarium" scare you. You're the boss. Picture a tiny garden, beautiful and well-kept, sealed in a transparent glass or plastic container. That's a terrarium. What's it used for? They are for keeping plants or terrestrial or semi-terrestrial animals inside the house. People do this for decoration purposes, to make their home look cool, for scientific observation, or for plant or animal breeding like you're doing for your pet. Here's how to pick the perfect terrarium for your pet:

Get a Glass Box with Air Holes. Look for a clear container made of glass. It needs holes in the top or sides to let fresh air in and old air out. Think of it like tiny windows for your pet to breathe.

It Should Have an Easy-Open Door. Get a terrarium that opens from the front like a mini fridge. It makes it far easier to clean and care for your pet without reaching all the way in.

Does It Have an Escape-Proof Lid? The top must be secure so your curious critters can't climb out and explore on their own. This lid also keeps the temperature and humidity just right inside.

Make the Home a Rocky Fun Zone. Fill the terrarium with cool stuff like rocks, branches, and plants. Think of it like a jungle gym for your pet to hide in, climb on, strut around, and have fun exploring.

It Should Have a Shady Spot. Don't put the terrarium where the wind blows or the sun shines directly on it. This can make it too hot or cold for your pet. So, find a cozy corner away from the window for their mini home.

Size and Space Requirements

Size Matters: Your dragon needs enough room to roam, not just sit still. Think "skateboard park," not "shoebox."

Baby Dragons: For little guys, a 20-gallon tank is okay to start, but they'll grow fast.

Big Dragons: When your dragon's all grown up, they'll need at least a 40-gallon tank or even bigger. As with newborn babies, when they're tiny, they are placed in baby beds and cribs, but as they grow older, the crib no longer fits them. It is the same with bearded dragons. They need a bigger home when they grow. Imagine a comfy apartment, not a tiny studio.

Length Is Important: Bearded dragons like to run around on the ground, not climb walls. So, the longer the tank, the better. It shouldn't be designed like a phone booth. Think about it for a moment. Will you be comfortable living in a square box with no space to move around? No, right? So, don't do that to your pet. Make sure it has enough room to explore.

Substrate Choices

Decorating your bearded dragon's new home is fun, but picking the "ground cover" is very important. It's like choosing the rug for your room – it has to be safe, easy to clean, and comfy for your pet. This way, your dragon can chill, dig, and explore without getting stuck or sick. A happy dragon needs a happy "floor," so pick the right one. Here are things you should think about when picking the right "ground cover" for your bearded dragon:

Put Safety First: Don't use anything your dragon could accidentally eat and get sick from. Don't bother using sand

and gravel. They're like tiny Legos your dragon might swallow by accident.

It Should Be Easy to Clean: You'll be cleaning this terrarium often, so choose something that doesn't take forever. The faster you can clean the dragon's home, the happier you'll be.

Foot-Friendly Options: Carpet, paper towels, tiles, or shelf liners are good choices. Imagine comfy shoes, not prickly sandals.

Skip the Sand: Sand and gravel can get stuck in your dragon's tummy and make them very sick. Avoid them.

Temperature and Lighting Needs

Temperature Zones: Think of it like a "cool zone" and a "sun zone." The cool zone should be around 75-80°F (24-27°C), perfect for relaxing. But your dragon needs a warm spot to bask in, like a mini beach.

Sun Zone Heat: Let the temperature where the dragon will be basking mostly be around 95-105°F (35-40°C). Imagine a heat lamp or special heater like a tiny sun keeping things warm.

Vitamin D Light: Dragons need special UVB light, like tiny suns, to stay healthy. It's like a magic ray that helps them develop strong bones. Get a full-spectrum UVB light for your dragon's home. Ask the adults around you for help to find the right light.

Temperature Check: Use a thermometer like a doctor to regularly check the temperature in both zones. If it's too hot or cold, adjust the heater or move the thermometer to find a spot your dragon will love.

Essential Accessories and Hideouts

Climbing Fun: Picture a gym set up inside a jungle. Your pet needs activities to keep them fit. So, include platforms, branches, and rocks they can climb on and bask under their heat lamp. You know how lizards like to sunbathe on a rock or chill in a treehouse – bearded dragons like that, too.

The Dragon and Its Hideout: Dragons need to feel safe, so provide them with multiple hiding spots like caves, logs, or cardboard boxes (with awesome decorations). Think of a secret fort, not an open field.

Water Station: Give your dragon a shallow water dish for drinking or soaking in. Something small enough to pass as a birdbath, not a swimming pool – keep it shallow to avoid accidents.

Plantastic Vibes: Decorate their place with fake or live (non-toxic) plants. Your pet's home should look like a mini rainforest, not a barren desert. Plants make it look cool and help keep the air fresh.

Add a Hammock to the Mix: They love chilling in hammocks, so stick one in a cool corner away from their heat lamp, like the opposite side of the tank. Do this, and your dragon will thank you.

Setting up your bearded dragon's crib isn't only about making it look cool (although that's part of it). You need things to keep them happy and healthy. The glass or plastic box should include climbing platforms, branches, and rocks for exploring. Give your pet the perfect home, and you'll be glad you did. Remember, this is only a guide to creating the perfect home for your bearded dragon. So, don't hesitate to ask a pet expert for tips to make your dragon's home the ultimate hangout.

Chapter 4: Feeding and Nutrition

Imagine a world without food, where people's stomachs growl in greeting one another, and there is no food or diet to sustain families. What do you think would happen to the human race? It's terrifying to think about, right? What about a world where, although people have something to eat, they don't get proper nutritional value from the food? In that world, you would surely see most people looking weird - some with diseases that don't seem to heal fast enough, some with weak bones and poor immunity systems, and some with digestive system problems.

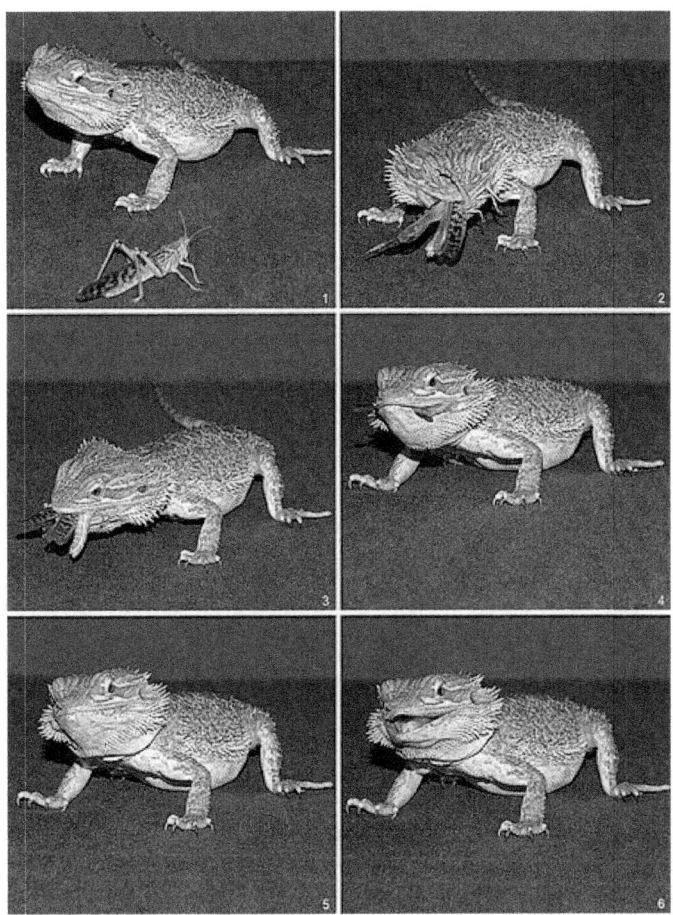

12. *Bearded dragon eating. Source: André Karwath aka Aka, CC BY-SA 2.5 <https://creativecommons.org/licenses/by-sa/2.5>, via Wikimedia Commons. https://commons.wikimedia.org/wiki/File:Feeding_a_Bearded_Dragon.jpg*

Food is dearly essential to living things, from humans like you to animals and plants. It is one of the basic needs of survival. Good food is like a step up. Everyone needs it to live a healthy life. So, in this chapter, you'll learn about the eating habits and diets of the bearded dragon. You'll be given tips on how to choose the right food for your pet. You can't just feed it with anything that comes to your mind. They have their own unique diet plans.

Another consideration is portion control. Your pet doesn't need to eat a whole horse at once. It'll choke and constipate. This chapter will also teach you how to properly schedule your bearded dragon's feeding and dish out a portion just right for them. For all of this and more, move on to the next section.

Understanding Bearded Dragon Diets

These tiny dinosaurs are omnivores, meaning they will happily munch on plants or meat. In the wild, they munch on insects, small rodents, and various plants. But when they're pets, their diet changes a little. You need to understand certain things to keep them healthy and happy. Your dragon is counting on you to be a good parent, ensuring it's always properly fed.

What Do Bearded Dragons Eat?

Bearded dragons love a good meal of insects. They eat crickets, mealworms, and even roaches. But they also need fruit and veggies to stay healthy. Some of their favorites are apples, carrots, and leafy greens like kale. They need a bit of calcium, which they can get from a special powder you sprinkle on their food.

Unlike their wild cousins, who roam free and hunt for food, pet bearded dragons live a more relaxed life. So they don't need as much exercise or food to stay healthy. Too much food can make them overweight, which is bad for their health. So, like being the responsible adult – you must watch what your dragon eats even though they'd happily gobble down anything you put in front of them.

Choosing the Right Food

Choosing the right food for your bearded dragon is vital. You want to make sure they're getting all the necessary nutrients.

Insects

When it comes to insects, variety is key. Don't just feed your bearded dragon crickets all the time. Mix it up with mealworms, roaches, or even silkworms. Make sure the insects are not too big for your bearded dragon. A good rule of thumb is never to feed them anything bigger than the space between their eyes.

Insect Buffet

They love bugs. Dragons are natural-born hunters, so live insects are their favorites. Think crickets, mealworms, roaches (if you're brave), locusts, and silkworms. But remember, variety is key. Don't stick to only one type.

Size Matters. Imagine an insect bigger than your dragon's eye – scary, right? That's why insects should be bite-sized, never exceeding the space between their eyes. This prevents choking and digestive issues.

Gut Healthy Treats. Gut health is crucial for your dragon. Offer gut-loaded insects, meaning you feed them nutritious foods like fruits and veggies beforehand. This helps your dragon get extra nutrients from their insect "dinner."

Don't Feed Them These Bugs:

Wild Bugs: This includes creepy crawlies you find outside, in your house, or at a bait shop. You never know what they might have been munching on, and it could make your dragon horribly sick.

Zombie Bugs: Dead insects are a big no-no. They can have bacteria that will make your dragon terribly ill. Think of them like rotten treasure – it's not worth the risk.

Elderbugs: These little red guys might look harmless, but they are actually toxic to dragons. Just imagine them as tiny dragon-poisonous apples.

Glowing Bugs: Fireflies and other insects that glow in the dark are a big NOPE. They can be poisonous or have parasites that harm your dragon. They are like glowing danger signs.

Venomous Friends: This includes insects that can sting or bite you, like bees, wasps, and scorpions. They are not part of a balanced dragon diet.

Worms

Remember those wiggly friends you used to dig up in the dirt? Well, some worms are tasty treats for your bearded dragon. But choose wisely because not all worms are created equal:

Protein Powerhouses:

- **Butter Worms:** They are protein shakes for your dragon. Full of calcium and protein, they're a great addition to your dragon's regular bug meals.
- **Phoenix Worms:** Packed with protein and calcium, these little guys are like tiny dragon snacks.

- **Silkworms:** These can pass as a healthy candy bar for your dragon. Silkworms have protein, moisture, and essential minerals like calcium and potassium.

Treat Time Worms:

- **Earthworms:** They are not the most popular, but they offer calcium and hydration. Just rinse them off first to get rid of dirt.
- **Mealworms:** These are like adult-only cookies for your dragon. They're hard to digest for babies but okay for grown-ups in small amounts.

Fruits and Veggies

Fruits and veggies should make up about 20% of an adult bearded dragon's diet. Stick to fruits and veggies low in phosphorus, like apples, carrots, and leafy greens. Avoid feeding them lettuce, though, as it doesn't have much nutritional value. Use these tips when picking out fruits and veggies they'll love.

- **Plant Power:** Don't forget the greens. Think of them like vitamins and minerals in delicious, crunchy form.
- **Tasty Choices:** Apple slices, carrot sticks, and leafy greens like kale and collard are dragon-approved. Avoid iceberg lettuce, though. It's like junk food for them – not very nutritious.
- **Hydration Station:** Even though they get water from their food, a shallow dish is essential for drinking and soaking. But make sure it's shallow enough to avoid drowning accidents.

Supplements

Your little bearded buddy needs calcium to keep their bones strong. You can buy a special calcium powder to sprinkle on their food. They also need vitamin D3 to help them absorb the calcium. Some bearded dragons can get enough D3 from their lights, but others might need a supplement.

Feeding Schedule and Portion Control

Feeding your bearded dragon the correct amount of food at the right time is as important as what you feed them. Knowing when and how much to feed is like knowing how much fuel to put in your bike. Overdo it, and you get problems. You don't want that.

How Often Should I Feed My Bearded Dragon?

Baby Dragons: Tiny Tummies have big appetites. Growing babies need more frequent meals – 2-3 times a day. But don't keep refilling the plate – let them finish their food before offering more.

Adult Dragons: Be strict on giving them a once-a-day feast. Grown-ups don't need as much as babies. One meal a day is enough. Remember the size rule – no giant bugs. Remember, it's very important to let them finish eating. Don't rush them, please. They don't like that.

How Much Should I Feed My Bearded Dragon?

The amount of food your bearded dragon needs is determined by their age. Babies should eat as many small insects as they can in 5-10 minutes. Adults should eat about 50-75 small insects per week. Remember, the insects should be no bigger than the space between your bearded dragon's eyes.

Feeding your bearded dragon a balanced diet is key to keeping them fit and strong. Remember to provide a variety of insects and low-phosphorus fruits and veggies. Don't forget the calcium supplement. Different dragons have different needs based on age, health, and activity level. Consult your pet expert if you need advice on feeding your bearded dragon. With the proper knowledge and a little imagination, you can be a pro dragon chef, whipping up nutritious and delicious meals that keep your scaly friend happy and healthy for years. If you want to get fancy, try making your own dragon food mixes with chopped veggies, insects, and calcium powder. But ensure you research and use safe ingredients. You're good to go.

Chapter 5: Health and Wellness

Elvis always had a snotty nose. The boy and the flu are like E and F in the alphabet order. They always go together. His mother realized this when he was three and took him to the hospital for a check-up. They found out he had allergies that caused him to suffer from the common cold frequently. After the health issue was diagnosed, Elvis and his mom battled his allergies with prescriptions from the doctor until the boy got better. He can now walk around without fear of falling sick on a whim. Like Elvis, people, and even animals fall sick sometimes. Plants, too. But like with Elvis and his mom, once the cause of the illness is traced, it can be tackled effectively.

13. A healthy bearded dragon is kept at the right temperature. Source: André Karwath aka Aka, CC BY-SA 2.5 <https://creativecommons.org/licenses/by-sa/2.5>, via Wikimedia Commons. https://commons.wikimedia.org/wiki/File:Bearded_Dragon_in_te rrarium.jpg

This chapter is about the health and wellness of the bearded dragon. It includes understanding their diet, recognizing health signs, and knowing when to visit the vet. They, too, can fall sick and suffer weird diseases. So, as the parent of your little pet, you need to be on the lookout for anything that is out of the ordinary. You must watch the animal closely because it has the uncanny ability to hide how it feels. In the wild, they hide signs of being sick or hurt because predators are always looking for weak prey. So, learning about their health problems, even if your dragon seems fine, is essential. They are such good actors they deserve a Golden Globe Award.

Common Health Issues

Metabolic Bone Disease (MBD)

The bones of your bearded dragon are like a bicycle wheel's wheel. They give the wheel structure and balance. The dragon's bones need the proper nutrition to stay strong and work properly. If they don't get it, Metabolic Bone Disease (MBD) will set in. It's when their bones don't get enough calcium and vitamin D3, which are vital nutrients for bone health.

The bad news is that if your dragon has MBD, their bones will become weak and fragile, like a rusty bike frame. It makes it hard for them to move around, climb, or even eat. They might have telltale signs like:

1. **Soft Bones:** Their legs look wobbly, or their jaw seems squishy.

2. **Trouble Moving:** Climbing rocks or basking might become a struggle.

3. **Jaw Problems:** Their jaw might look swollen or have an underbite, making it hard to eat.

The good news? You can prevent this vibe-killer, MBD. Like you ensure your bike gets regular maintenance, give your dragon these essentials:

1. **Calcium Powder:** Sprinkle this dust-looking material on their food, like putting oil in a car engine. It works like magic.

2. **UVB Light:** This will provide them with artificial sunshine for their bones. They need it. So, get a special bulb for their tank.

Respiratory Infections

Picture your dragon sneezing and snotting, like poor Elvis. It's got a bad cold. This is a respiratory infection. It happens when their tank is too cold and damp, like a stuffy basement. Brrr. They would break out of there if they could. Why? This is what happens:

1. **Their Breathing Gets Weird:** They might wheeze, puff their throat, or have an open mouth like they're gasping for air.
2. **Snot Happens:** You might see bubbles or discharge coming from their nose, like when Elvis had a runny nose.
3. **Food Becomes Boring:** They might lose their appetite because it's hard to eat and breathe at the same time.

Yellow Fungus

Do you know what mold is? It's a fungal growth that feeds off the dampness and decay, helping to break down things like leaves and wood. Your bearded dragon has a bad case of mold in this illness. Yellow fungus is a serious infection that can spread deep under the skin and to their organs if left untreated. Don't be afraid. You can save your friend. What you should know about the yellow fungus:

1. **It's Ugly:** The fungus turns their scales yellow, and as it worsens, the scales can fall off, leaving their skin sore and raw.
2. **It's Sneaky:** Bearded dragons are good at hiding when they're sick, so you must be a detective and watch for any changes.

3. **It's Serious:** But the good news is, the sooner you catch it, the easier it is to treat. Like with a splinter, treating it early before it gets super-infected is better.

So, what do you do about it?

1. Watch out for yellow crusts on their skin, especially if they're growing or spreading.
2. Look out for changes in behavior, like not eating or acting grumpy.
3. If you see anything suspicious, don't wait. Take your pet to the vet right away.

Impaction

So, what if you were told that the bearded dragon could eat a giant burger? You would disagree, right? Now, imagine your bearded dragon trying to eat that burger. It would look hilarious trying to guzzle that down. This food that gets stuck is called impaction. It happens whenever they swallow something too big or hard to poop out, like a tiny car stuck in a small tunnel. Here's how to spot this issue:

1. **Beardie Is on Poop Hold-on:** Your dragon might not poop for days, even though they seem like they're trying really hard.
2. **Belly Bloat:** Their belly might puff up like a party balloon, but not in a fun way.
3. **Food Becomes 'Bleh':** They might lose their appetite because their tummy feels all packed and backed up.

Not cool, right? If you see these signs, take your dragon to the vet immediately. They can help with the problem and get things moving again.

In case you feel up for a home remedy, that's alright. You can solve the poop trouble. Here's how:

1. **Don't Give Them Big Meat:** Only feed your dragon things smaller than the space between their eyes, like bite-sized snacks, not whole pizzas.

2. **Skip the Tough Stuff:** Avoid foods like hard mealworms or crickets that are hard to digest. Think soft and chewable, like yummy greens and veggies.

Signs of a Healthy Bearded Dragon

Do you want to see the coolest reptile on the block? Yeah, it's that healthy-looking bearded buddy. You can spot a happy and thriving bearded dragon by:

1. **They're Bouncing Off the Walls (Well, Their Enclosure Walls):** A healthy dragon is like a tiny explorer, always checking things out and moving around. Curious and alive.

2. **Their Eyes Are Like Disco Balls:** Bright, clear eyes with no cloudiness or gunk mean your dragon sees the world perfectly. They are perfectly fine. No blurry vision here.

3. **Not Too Skinny, Not Too Fat:** Their body should be firm and well-rounded, not bony or bulging with fat.

4. **Smooth Skin:** Their skin should be flawless - no weird bumps, sores, or dry patches.

5. **They Eat Like a Champ:** They should gobble down their food with gusto, not turn up their nose like a

picky eater. Your bearded dragon should show a mini "pizza party" excitement for every meal.

6. **Regular Bathroom Breaks:** Like you, they gotta go sometimes. Regularly pooping shows their digestive system is working like a charm. No constipation is allowed.

Routine Care and Veterinary Visits

You don't shower your pet with love and care for a while and then stop. That's cruel. If the tables were turned, you wouldn't like that, would you? Routine care is important for keeping your bearded dragon healthy. You should practice taking care of them regularly until it becomes second nature. This routine includes cleaning their tank, handling them gently, and checking their health.

Cleaning Their Tank

Bearded dragons are tidy creatures. They don't like living in a dirty tank. You should clean their tank at least once a week by removing poop, uneaten food, and shed skin. Also, clean their water and food dish every day.

Handling Your Bearded Dragon

Your bearded dragon loves being handled, but be gentle. Always support their body when you pick them up. Never grab them by the tail, as this can hurt them. Also, wash your hands before and after handling your bearded dragon to prevent spreading germs.

Checking Their Health

You should check your bearded dragon's health every day. Look for signs of sickness, like not eating, being lazy, or having runny poop. If you see anything weird, take your bearded dragon to the vet.

Visiting the Vet

Even if your bearded dragon seems healthy, they should still see the vet once a year for a check-up. The vet will check for hidden health issues and give your bearded dragon a general health check. They can answer questions about caring for your bearded dragon.

It's easier to avoid problems than fix them later. If you see any of these signs, don't wait. The sooner you act, the better your dragon's chance of shaking off yucky or disturbing disease and staying healthy and happy. Ask your parents or a pet store expert for advice on your dragon's needs. Keep this up, and your bearded friend will love you.

Chapter 6: Fun Facts and Quirky Behavior

Brace yourselves for a wild ride as you dig into the juicy tidbits about the one and only Bearded Dragon. This chapter is your backstage pass to the lizard extravaganza, where you'll learn about their bizarre behaviors, explore their cool physiology, and highlight the quirky stuff that makes these little dudes real rockstars. Whether you're a hardcore reptile geek or just dipping your toes into the scaly scene, hang tight as you go through the secrets that make bearded dragons one of the most visually striking species in the reptile world.

14. Bearded dragons can be funny! Source: Whosagoodlizard, CC BY-SA 4.0 <https://creativecommons.org/licenses/by-sa/4.0>, via Wikimedia Commons. https://commons.wikimedia.org/wiki/File:Chef_Lenny_the_Lizard_on_Doughnut_Day.jpg

Unusual Behaviors Explained

Digging and Burrowing

Bearded dragons like to dig and burrow in their substrate (the stuff at the bottom of their tank). This behavior is similar to making a cozy home. They might dig to find a cooler or warmer spot or to hide. It's their way of creating a comfy space to relax.

Basking Rituals

Dragons love to bask under a heat lamp or in the sunlight. This practice helps them warm their bodies, stay healthy, and get much-needed energy.

Glass Surfing

Dragons might slide or rub against their tank's walls. They do this to explore the area when they are curious about what's outside or are simply trying to get your attention. Sometimes, it's their way of saying they want more space or a change in their environment.

Tail Curling

Bearded dragons curl their tail around things or themselves. It is often a sign of feeling secure or cozy. They also do tail curling when they're sleeping or just chilling.

Gape Threat Display

Sometimes, bearded dragons open their mouths wide, showing their black insides. It's a self-defense mechanism. They do this if they feel threatened or want to ward off potential danger. It's a true display of its intimidating side.

Elevated Arm Display

Dragons might raise one of their arms, especially during interaction. This is a social move, and you might see them doing the maneuver more often. It's their way of communicating with other dragons, saying they're friendly, or establishing their space.

Bobbing While Walking

Bearded Dragons might bob their heads when walking. It's a mix of walking and head-bobbing - they might do it when they're exploring or feeling playful.

The more you study the behavior of bearded dragons, the more you'll understand these unusual behaviors are there for several reasons. Understanding these actions can make you better understand their needs and emotions.

For example, head-bobbing, arm-waving, and elevated arm displays show how they interact socially and express themselves to fellow dragons or you.

The digging, burrowing, or changing their color (puffing and darkening) is to adapt to their surroundings. This behavior also helps regulate their body temperature, find comfortable hiding spots, or protect themselves from threats. Likewise, tail-curling might indicate a sense of security or relaxation, while gape threat displays are a way of expressing discomfort.

Understanding these behaviors can educate you to properly care for and create a suitable environment for your dragon's physical and emotional needs. It's about learning their unique language and ensuring they lead happy and healthy lives in their terrarium.

Fun Facts That Surprise Even Adults

Third Eye

Bearded dragons have a third eye called the parietal eye on the top of their heads. Although it doesn't see like a regular eye, it can detect changes in light and shadow, helping them sense predators from above.

Antibacterial Licking

Bearded dragons have a unique way of keeping their environment clean. They use their tongues to lick surfaces, which have antibacterial properties. This behavior helps them maintain hygiene and prevent infections.

Color-Changing Magic

While bearded dragons can't change colors like chameleons, they exhibit color changes. Their skin can darken or lighten based on temperature, mood, and health.

Rapid Growth Spurts

These reptiles are known for their impressive growth rates. During their first year, they can grow from a tiny hatchling to a foot-long adult. These bearded dragons thrive well when provided the required care.

Gentle Personalities

Despite their intimidating name, bearded dragons are often docile and gentle. They are famous for their calm demeanor, making them excellent reptile companions.

Life Expectancy Wisdom

Bearded dragons have a long lifespan for reptiles. They can live from 10 to 15 years or even longer with proper care. It's like having a scaly friend who can be a lifelong companion.

Vocal Communication

Bearded dragons might not bark or meow but communicate through various sounds. They can make gentle squeaks, hisses, or a beard puffing sound.

These fun facts highlight the incredible and surprising nature of bearded dragons, putting them on top of the list of fascinating members of the reptile kingdom. Whether you're a first-time dragon owner or a seasoned reptile enthusiast, knowing these facts adds an extra layer of information about bearded dragons.

Unique Traits That Make Bearded Dragons Special

Cool Calmness

Bearded dragons are renowned for their calm and easygoing demeanor. Their temperament and tolerant attitude to handling make them stand out as gentle and personable reptilian companions.

Playful Bobbing

This rhythmic head movement is a signature trait of the bearded dragon. It seems like a dance and often happens when they're feeling active or joyful, adding a touch of playfulness to their character.

Tail Language

The way bearded dragons use their tails goes beyond balance. They might curl their tails around themselves or objects, conveying comfort or ownership.

Distinctive Markings

Bearded dragons have unique patterns and markings on their scales. These distinctive features make each dragon unique, creating diversity among the species.

Sun Soaking Rituals

Bearded dragons are sun enthusiasts. Their ritual of basking in the sun's warmth or under a heat lamp isn't only about temperature regulation. It's like they're enjoying a spa day, soaking up the energy they need to thrive.

Graceful Glass Climbing

Bearded dragons might surprise you with their climbing abilities. They can navigate and explore vertical surfaces, walk on many textures, and showcase a gracefulness not often associated with ground-dwelling reptiles.

Customizable Color Palette

As you already know, bearded dragons come in several colors, and their ability to change shades based on mood and environment adds an extra layer of fascination.

Curiosity and Exploration

Bearded dragons are naturally curious creatures. Their tendency to explore their surroundings, with a keen interest in new objects, makes them curious adventurers within their enclosures.

Chapter 7: Engaging Activities for Kids

In this chapter, you won't just read about bearded dragons but learn how to engage with them actively. You'll discover a range of experiences that go beyond these pages. Throughout this chapter, you'll learn about safe handling techniques and how to build trust and form lasting connections with your scaly companions. Later, you'll read about various DIY activities and interactive games for your bearded dragon, making your interactions fun and safe.

15. You can establish trust between you and a bearded dragon. Source: Emőke Dénes, CC BY-SA 4.0 <https://creativecommons.org/licenses/by-sa/4.0>, via Wikimedia Commons. https://commons.wikimedia.org/wiki/File:Pogona_vitticeps_-_London_7.jpg

Safe Handling Techniques

Safe handling of bearded dragons is crucial for the dragon's well-being and the handler's safety. Here's an in-depth guide to safe handling techniques:

Prepare the Environment

Secure the Enclosure: Before handling, ensure the bearded dragon's enclosure is escape-proof. Close any openings and make sure there are no potential hazards in the area.

Comfortable Temperature: Ensure the room is at a temperature that prevents stress for the dragon.

Wash Your Hands

Wash your hands thoroughly with mild soap and water before handling to remove scents or residues that might stress the dragon. The best way is to create a hand-washing routine before and after interacting with the dragon.

Approaching the Dragon

Slow and Gentle Movements: Approach your bearded dragon slowly and use calm, gentle movements. Abrupt actions can startle them.

Lift and Support

Support the Body: When picking up the dragon, support its body properly to avoid stress on its limbs. Place one hand under its chest and the other supporting its hindquarters.

Avoid Grabbing the Tail: Bearded dragons can drop their tails as a defense mechanism, so avoid grabbing or pulling on the tail.

Reading Body Language

Respect Signals: Be aware of the dragon's body language. If it shows signs of stress (flattening body, darkening color, hissing), it may prefer not to be handled at that moment.

Handling Time

Start Gradually: For new or young dragons, start with short handling sessions and gradually increase the duration as they become more accustomed.

Respect Individual Preferences: Some dragons may enjoy longer handling sessions, while others prefer shorter, more frequent interactions.

Avoid Sudden Movements

Minimize Startling: Sudden movements can startle bearded dragons. Move slowly and predictably to help them feel secure.

Return to the Enclosure

Gently Place Down: When returning the dragon to its enclosure, lower it gently to avoid sudden drops.

Children and Supervision

Supervise Interactions: If children are handling the dragon, ensure close supervision to prevent accidental drops or rough handling. Teach children to be gentle and calm.

Respect Individual Personalities:

Recognize Preferences: Bearded dragons, like people, have different personalities. Some may enjoy frequent handling, while others prefer solitude. Respect and cater to their individual preferences.

Creating DIY enrichment activities for your bearded dragon is a fantastic way to keep them engaged and stimulated. Here are some DIY enrichment ideas to add excitement to your dragon's environment:

DIY Enrichment Ideas

Foraging Stations

Purpose: Encourage natural hunting behaviors.

Materials:
- Cardboard tubes
- Small, safe containers

- Live or fake plants
- Dubia roaches or crickets (or other appropriate live feeders)

Instructions:
1. Create a foraging area by placing cardboard tubes and containers throughout the enclosure.
2. Hide live feeders or favorite veggies inside the tubes and containers.
3. Your dragon will enjoy exploring and hunting for its food.

Climbing Structures

Purpose: Promote physical activity and exercise.

Materials:
- Sturdy branches or driftwood
- Non-toxic ropes
- Reptile-safe glue
- Artificial plants for decoration

Instructions:
1. Secure branches together to create a stable structure.
2. Use ropes to create climbing paths.
3. Add artificial plants for aesthetics.
4. Place the structure in your dragon's enclosure for climbing and exploring.

Custom Digging Box

Purpose: Satisfy natural burrowing instincts.

Materials:

- Plastic storage container
- Coconut coir or topsoil
- Small objects for burying

Instructions:

1. Fill the container with coconut coir or topsoil.
2. Bury small objects or treats for your dragon to discover.
3. This provides a space for digging and burrowing.

Mirror Play

Purpose: Stimulate visual engagement.

Materials:

- Small, safe mirror
- Velcro strips

Instructions:

1. Attach the mirror to the enclosure wall using Velcro.
2. Bearded dragons often enjoy interacting with their reflection.

Homemade Puzzle Feeder

Purpose: Mental stimulation during feeding.

Materials:

- Clear plastic container with a lid
- Craft knife
- Dubia roaches or mealworms

Instructions:
1. Cut small openings in the container lid.
2. Place live feeders inside.
3. Your dragon will need to figure out how to access the feeders.

Sensory Bin

Purpose: Engage senses through exploration.

Materials:
- Shallow plastic container
- Safe substrates like shredded paper or sand
- Safe objects for exploration (smooth rocks, plastic toys)

Instructions:
1. Fill the container with substrates and add safe objects.
2. Your dragon can explore and interact with different textures.

Remember to observe your bearded dragon during these activities to ensure they are comfortable and enjoying the enrichment. These DIY ideas provide mental and physical stimulation, nurturing a happy and healthy dragon.

Educational Games about Bearded Dragons

Engaging in educational games is a fantastic way to learn more about bearded dragons while having fun. Here are a few educational games that will entertain and deepen your understanding of these fascinating reptiles:

Dragon Bingo

Objective: Learn about different aspects of bearded dragon care and behavior.

Materials:

- Bingo cards with images or terms related to bearded dragons
- Markers or counters

Instructions:

1. Create bingo cards with pictures or terms like "basking," "shedding," or "insects."
2. Call out descriptions or characteristics, and players mark the corresponding spaces.
3. The first to get a line shouts, "Dragon Bingo!"

Dragon Trivia Board Game

Objective: Test and expand your knowledge of bearded dragons.

Materials:

- A board with spaces for questions
- Trivia cards with bearded dragon facts
- Game pieces

Instructions:

1. Players move across the board by answering trivia questions.
2. Correct answers advance the player, and the first to reach the finish line wins.

Habitat Builder

Objective: Understand the components of a bearded dragon's habitat.

Materials:

- Paper or cardboard.
- Art supplies.
- Images of various habitat elements.

Instructions:

1. Draw or cut out pictures of different habitat components (basking spot, hiding place, water dish).
2. Create a landscape on paper or cardboard, placing the elements in the correct locations.

Behavior Charades

Objective: Act out and guess bearded dragon behaviors.

Materials:

- Behavior cards with actions like "head-bobbing" or "basking."
- Timer

Instructions:

1. Players draw a card and act out the behavior without speaking.
2. Others try to guess the behavior before the timer runs out.

Life Cycle Puzzles

Objective: Understand the life stages of bearded dragons.

Materials:

- Images or drawings representing different life stages.
- Cardboard or puzzle pieces.

Instructions:

1. Create puzzle pieces with images of bearded dragons at various life stages.
2. Assemble the puzzle to learn about their life cycle.

These educational games make learning about bearded dragons interactive and enjoyable. Whether playing solo or with friends, these activities will deepen your understanding of these incredible reptiles in a fun and entertaining way.

Chapter 8: Frequently Asked Questions

This chapter includes comprehensive Frequently Asked Questions (FAQs) as your troubleshooting guide on this scaly expedition.

16. Bearded dragons can eat pears! Source: Multiphrenic, CC BY-SA 3.0 <https://creativecommons.org/licenses/by-sa/3.0>, via Wikimedia Commons. https://commons.wikimedia.org/wiki/File:Bearded_dragon_eating_pear.jpg

Addressing Common Concerns

Q: How can I ensure my bearded dragon is healthy?

A: Regularly monitor its activity levels, eating habits, and the condition of its scales. Signs of lethargy, changes in appetite, or abnormal behaviors signal a closer examination and, if needed, consultation with a vet.

Q: What should I feed my bearded dragon, and how often?

A: Bearded dragons require a varied diet, including insects, leafy greens, and vegetables. Feed them appropriate portion sizes daily, adjusting based on age and health. Make sure you include an adequate calcium-to-phosphorus ratio in their diet and include multivitamin supplements as the vet recommends.

Q: How do I set up the ideal habitat for my bearded dragon?

A: The enclosure you set up must include proper safety, lighting, and temperature. Always add a substrate suitable for burrowing, and incorporate hiding spots, basking areas, and enriching elements, like climbing structures, to keep your scaly friends engaged.

Q: What are common behavioral cues, and how can I interpret them?

A: Bearded dragons communicate through behaviors like head-bobbing, tail-curling, and glass surfing. Understanding these cues builds trust and addresses their needs, whether for attention, exploration, or relaxation.

Q: Is breeding bearded dragons a complex process, and what should I be aware of?

A: Breeding involves understanding the mating behaviors, egg-laying, and caring for gravid females. Furthermore, being prepared for the responsibilities of breeding is crucial. Consult with experienced breeders or vets for guidance.

Q: How can I safely handle my bearded dragon and build a bond with it?

A: Practice slow and gentle movements, supporting its body during handling. Gradually increase the handling time and pay attention to its body language. Building trust is a patient process requiring positive interactions.

Q: What are common health concerns, and how should I respond in emergencies?

A: Although there are various health concerns, the most notable ones include respiratory infections, metabolic bone disease, and parasites. Regular vet check-ups are essential. Have a reptile-friendly vet's contact information for emergencies and be prepared to provide immediate care.

Troubleshooting Tips for New Bearded Dragon Owners

For new dragon owners navigating through potential hiccups, here are troubleshooting tips for common issues to make this experience smooth and enjoyable.

Inadequate Appetite

A bearded dragon's tummy is sensitive to temperature. Whenever there's a temperature fluctuation in the enclosure, there's a high chance the bearded dragon will develop digestion issues. Besides ensuring the temperature is right, switch the food source to live feeders and fresh vegetables to see whether the issue persists. However, if the issue is not resolved, consult a vet for a health check.

Difficulty Shedding

Set up a shedding box with damp moss to help the process. Keep proper humidity levels in the enclosure for the best results. Don't hesitate to contact the vet if the issue persists.

Changes in Behavior

Monitor for signs of stress, illness, or discomfort. Check for changes in the environment, handling routines, or recent additions to the enclosure that might be causing stress.

Refusal to Eat Vegetables

Try different vegetables and presentation styles. Some dragons prefer finely chopped or grated veggies. Gradually introduce vegetables into their diet to encourage acceptance.

Inconsistent Bowel Movements

Ensure a proper balance of diet, including fiber from vegetables.

Glass Surfing

Assess your dragon's enclosure for potential stressors, such as reflections or unfamiliar items. Ensure it has proper hiding spots and consider adjusting the lighting. Glass surfing might also indicate a desire for more physical or mental stimulation.

Reluctance to Bask

Check the temperature gradient in the enclosure. Ensure the basking spot is at the correct temperature. If the dragon continues to avoid basking, consult a vet to rule out health concerns.

Aggressive Behavior

Evaluate the dragon's living environment, ensuring it has adequate space and hiding spots. If the aggression persists, reconsider your handling approach and consult an experienced reptile handler or vet.

Respiratory Symptoms

Monitor for signs of respiratory distress, such as wheezing or open-mouth breathing. Check for proper ventilation in the enclosure and consult a vet if the symptoms persist.

Overgrown Nails or Beak

Provide rough surfaces like rocks or branches for natural wear. If overgrowth occurs, consult a vet for guidance on safe trimming techniques.

Remember, each bearded dragon is unique, and troubleshooting may require a bit of patience and observation. If your concerns persist or you're unsure about a particular issue, seeking advice from a reptile-savvy vet is always the best step.

Additional Resources for Further Learning

Online Forums and Communities

Bearded Dragon Network (BDN): An active online community where you can share experiences, seek advice, and connect with other bearded dragon owners.

Reptile Forums: General reptile forums with dedicated sections for bearded dragons. Engage in discussions, ask questions, and learn from experienced keepers.

YouTube Channels

Clint's Reptiles: Clint provides educational and entertaining videos on various reptile species, including bearded dragons.

Dāv Kaufman: Follow Dāv as he shares his experiences and insights into the world of reptiles, including bearded dragons.

Veterinary Resources

Reptile Vets: Establish a relationship with a reptile-savvy vet. They can be your guide on health and nutrition and address medical concerns.

Reptile Expos

Check the local pet-friendly venues for reptile expos, which often feature expert breeders and enthusiasts. Attend these events for hands-on experience, to ask questions, and explore many resources.

Reputable Breeders

Reach out to reputable bearded dragon breeders for valuable information and guidance and to keep in contact with the reptile community.

From understanding their behaviors to engaging in activities and troubleshooting challenges, this book is a great option to expand your knowledge about these friendly and scaly dragons.

Conclusion

The information in this book is hard to memorize in a single read. You may need to read it at least twice to recollect certain important facts. You began with the introduction of the bearded dragon, where you were given a brief overview of the creature. It was followed by a more detailed description of its numerous varieties, characteristics, and habitat.

Then, you learned how to set up the perfect dragon home, from the temperature requirements to its bizarre hideouts. Since they are terrestrial creatures, their home would emulate the outside terrain. After that, it was time to understand its food requirements. You learned about its typical diet (veggies or insects) and feeding schedule (no more than once or twice a day).

The next chapter went into the health and wellness of your favorite pet. You were made aware of their common health issues and the solutions. Essential caring techniques were also included. Then, you learned a few fun facts about bearded dragons, along with their peculiar behavior that often depicts their emotional state.

Finally, a few exciting activities were given, from spectacular DIY ideas to intriguing educational games. The book ended with a series of frequently asked questions about bearded dragons.

Key Takeaways:

- A bearded dragon's beard is a collection of spikes or scales.
- They are territorial creatures with a love for rocky and heightened terrain.
- Their diet consists of a mixture of insects and vegetables.
- Their emotional state can be interpreted by the size and color of their beard.

References

Andreajn. (2020, March 10). 30 Surprising Bearded Dragon Facts You'd Never Imagined. Turn Your Curiosity into Discovery - Facts.net. https://facts.net/bearded-dragon-facts/

Are Bearded Dragons Venomous? Here's What You Need to Know. (n.d.). Dragon's Diet. https://dragonsdiet.com/blogs/dragon-care/are-bearded-dragons-venomous

Axelson, R., Rich, G., & Hess, L. (2009). Bearded Dragons - Diseases. Vca_corporate. https://vcahospitals.com/know-your-pet/bearded-dragons-diseases

Bearded Dragon Frequently Asked Questions. (n.d.). Www.thebeardeddragon.org. https://www.thebeardeddragon.org/bearded-dragon/faq

Bearded Dragon Fun Facts: 29 Cool Things You Probably Didn't Know abou. (n.d.). Dragon's Diet. https://dragonsdiet.com/blogs/dragon-care/29-bearded-dragon-fun-facts

Bearded Dragons. (n.d.). Bush Heritage Australia. https://www.bushheritage.org.au/species/bearded-dragons

Blake, M. (2022, April 21). Bearded Dragon Facts: Behavior, Characteristics & Care Tips | LoveToKnow Pets. LoveToKnow. https://www.lovetoknowpets.com/reptiles/bearded-dragon-facts

Briggs, H. (2020, August 1). The Ideal Bearded Dragon Habitat Setup (7 Steps). Reptile Direct. https://www.reptiledirect.com/bearded-dragon-habitat-setup/

Briggs, H. (2020, June 21). Bearded Dragon Bites: Why It Happens & Do They Hurt. Reptile Direct. https://www.reptiledirect.com/bearded-dragon-bite

Cantell, M. (2023, August 29). Breeding Bearded Dragons At Home: From Setup to Hatchlings. Bearded Dragon Guru. https://beardeddragonguru.com/breeding-bearded-dragons-at-home/

Care Sheet. (n.d.). Common Health Issues of Bearded Dragons | Bearded Dragon Care Sheet. Bearded Dragon Care 101. https://www.beardeddragoncare101.com/bearded-dragon-care-sheet/health-issues/

Collaborator, H. S. (2020, October 28). Bearded Dragon Tank Setup 101: How to Create the Best Home for Your New Pet. Dragon's Diet. https://dragonsdiet.com/blogs/dragon-care/bearded-dragon-tank-setup-101

Daniels, N. (2023, January 29). 8 Enrichment Activities for Bearded Dragons. PetHelpful. https://pethelpful.com/reptiles-amphibians/8-Enrichment-Activities-For-Bearded-Dragons

Dragon, T. B. (2022, September 13). Fun Bearded Dragon Facts & Information. Www.thebeardeddragon.org. https://www.thebeardeddragon.org/bearded-dragon/basics

England, J. (2018, June 19). Setting up a Bearded Dragon Habitat (Step-by-Step Guide). Reptile Advisor. https://www.reptileadvisor.com/bearded-dragon-habitat/

Finkelstein, A. (2014). Bearded Dragon Pet Care | Food, Environment, Supplements. TexVetPets. https://www.texvetpets.org/article/bearded-dragons-cold-blooded-companions/

Flanagan, M. (2020, April 2). The Complete Bearded Dragon Diet Plan. Dragon's Diet. https://dragonsdiet.com/blogs/dragon-care/the-complete-bearded-dragon-diet-plan

Green, J. (n.d.). The Bearded Dragon's Diet: What Can They Eat? | Falls Road Animal Hospital | Baltimore Vet. Www.fallsroad.com. https://www.fallsroad.com/site/tips-resources-blog-baltimore-vet/2022/01/14/bearded-dragon-diet#:~:text=Bearded%20Dragon%20Diet%20Plan&text=Since%20they%20are%20omnivores%2C%20they

Hinchee, L. E. (2022, March 22). How much fun can you have with your bearded dragon? Medium. https://lawrenceedwardhinchee.medium.com/how-much-fun-can-you-have-with-your-bearded-dragon-9cecf118779c

How to Play with a Bearded Dragon: Activities & Enrichment Ideas. (n.d.). Dragon's Diet. https://dragonsdiet.com/blogs/dragon-care/how-to-play-with-a-bearded-dragon-activities-enrichment-ideas

How to setup a Bearded Dragon Enclosure. (2023, December 2). Internet Reptile. https://internetreptile.com/blogs/reptile-learning-zone/how-to-setup-a-bearded-dragon-enclosure

Howtoanimal. (2022). 15 Signs That Your Bearded Dragon Is Healthy [Behaviors] – HowToAnimal. How to Animal . https://www.howtoanimal.com/signs-bearded-dragon-is-healthy/

https://wildlifeinformer.com/signs-your-bearded-dragon-is-happy/

https://www.facebook.com/thespruceofficial. (2019). How Do You Care for a Pet Bearded Dragon? The Spruce Pets. https://www.thesprucepets.com/bearded-dragons-as-pets-1236896

Informer, W. (2020, July 20). 13 Signs Your Bearded Dragon is Happy. Wildlife Informer.

Jones, E. (2022, November 12). How Can I Tell If My Bearded Dragon Is Healthy? 6 Signs. My Pet Reptiles. https://mypetreptiles.com/how-can-i-tell-if-my-bearded-dragon-is-healthy/

Max. (2010, October 29). Bearded Dragons - Facts And History. Youngzine. https://youngzine.org/u-write/u-report/bearded-dragons-facts-and-history

Méndez, A. (2018, November 3). Are you a bearded dragon-type of pet owner? Here are some tips. Pet LIfe Pro. https://www.petlifepro.com/2018/11/03/pet-life-pro-are-you-a-bearded-dragon-type-of-pet-owner/

Mills, A. (2023, March 20). Creating the Perfect Bearded Dragon Habitat: A Comprehensive Guide – Pet Safety Crusader. Pet Safety Crusader. http://www.petsafetycrusader.com/creating-the-perfect-bearded-dragon-habitat-a-comprehensive-guide/#:~:text=Size%20matters%3A%20Start%20with%20a

Newman, D. (2024, January 11). 5 Steps to Setting up a Bearded Dragon Habitat. PetHelpful. https://pethelpful.com/reptiles-amphibians/Set-Up-a-Bearded-Dragon-Habitat

Oddblog. (n.d.). How To Play With A Bearded Dragon (+What They Like For Play). Https://Oddlycutepets.com/. https://oddlycutepets.com/how-to-play-with-a-bearded-dragon/

petMD. (2017, August 28). 10 Bearded Dragon Facts You Should Know | petMD. Petmd.com. https://www.petmd.com/reptile/care/10-things-you-didnt-know-about-bearded-dragons

Rich, G., Hess, L., & Axelson, R. (2017). Bearded Dragons - Feeding. Vca_corporate. https://vcahospitals.com/know-your-pet/bearded-dragons-feeding

Schabacker, S. (2019, June 20). Bearded Dragons. National Geographic. https://www.nationalgeographic.com/animals/reptiles/facts/bearded-dragon

Sophia . (2022, January 3). Bearded Dragon Common Health Issues - The Bearded Dragon Blog. The Bearded Dragon Blog. https://thebeardeddragonblog.com/bearded-dragon-common-health-issues/

Stacey. (2019, July 28). 17 Must-Know Bearded Dragon Health Issues, Diseases, and Illnesses. Reptile.Guide. https://reptile.guide/bearded-dragon-health-issues/

Stacey. (2021, January 25). 10 Baby Bearded Dragon Care Mistakes New Owners Usually Make... Reptile.guide. https://reptile.guide/baby-bearded-dragon-care/

Team, B. (2017, November 1). How to Tame Baby Bearded Dragons. Pets on Mom.com. https://animals.mom.com/how-to-tame-baby-bearded-dragons-6663852.html

TeeRiddle. (2023, June 14). Bearded Dragon Care 101: A Beginner's Guide. PetHelpful. https://pethelpful.com/reptiles-amphibians/beginners-guide-keeping-bearded-dragon

The Bearded Dragon. (2022, September 7). Bearded Dragon Health, Illness, & Disease Symptoms. Www.thebeardeddragon.org. https://www.thebeardeddragon.org/bearded-dragon/health

The Ultimate Guide to Bearded Dragons. (2016). Zillarules.com. https://www.zillarules.com/articles/the-ultimate-guide-to-bearded-dragons

Types of Bearded Dragons» View Different Types, Colors, & Species. (2022, September 19). Www.thebeardeddragon.org. https://www.thebeardeddragon.org/bearded-dragon/types

Printed in Dunstable, United Kingdom